Genre Folktale

Essential Question
How can we understand nature?

Retold by Deborah November
Illustrated by Linda Bittner

PAIRED READ Why Bear Has a Short Tail . 17

CAST OF CHARACTERS

Little Turtle   Hunter 1
Turtle 1   Hunter 2
Turtle 2   Chief

LIFE OF THE TURTLE

Setting: A long time ago in Africa

Little Turtle: What a **lovely** day!

Turtle 1: Yes, life is good.

Turtle 2: We play in the tall grass.

Little Turtle: We always have **plenty** to eat.

STOP AND CHECK

Why do the turtles have good lives?

Turtle 1: Oh, no! **Hunters** are coming! Hide!

Turtle 2: Run, Little Turtle. **Hurry**!

> **STOP AND CHECK**
>
> Why does Little Turtle need to hurry?

SCENE 2
CAPTURE!

Setting: A path in the jungle

Hunter 1: We have you, Little Turtle!

Hunter 2: Don't even try to **dash** away.

Little Turtle: The hunters were so fast. I didn't have time to **holler** for help!

Little Turtle: I am sad the hunters caught me.

Hunter I: No talking, Little Turtle!

STOP AND CHECK

Who caught Little Turtle?

SCENE 3

THE VILLAGE

Setting: The hunters' village

Hunter 2: This is our village.

Little Turtle: I wonder if the village is like ours!

Chief: I am the village **chief**.

Little Turtle: I am just a turtle.

Chief: How shall we cook you?

Little Turtle: First, you have to take off my shell.

Chief: We can break your shell with sticks.

Little Turtle: That won't work. But you can throw me in the river. Then I will **drown**.

Chief: Good idea, Little Turtle. We will drown you! Then we can eat you!

> **STOP AND CHECK**
>
> What do the animals want to do with Little Turtle?

SCENE 4

ESCAPE!

Setting: The hunters' village

Little Turtle: Don't take out the cooking pots. I did not drown.

Hunter 1: Little Turtle tricked us!

Chief: Little Turtle can swim! He is getting away!

Little Turtle: I will stay in the water from now on. It's safer here.

Turtle 1: Little Turtle is back!

Turtle 2: Let's have a party!

Turtle 1: And that is why turtles live in water.

> **STOP AND CHECK**
> What did Little Turtle say after he landed in the river?

Summarize

Tell what happens in *Why Turtles Live in Water*. The chart may help you.

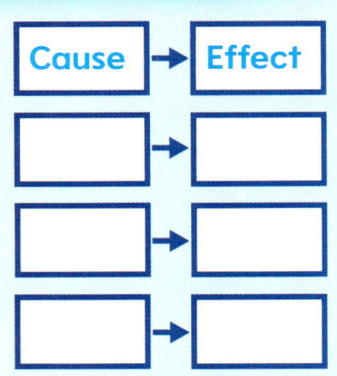

Text Evidence

1. Why does Chief throw Little Turtle in the water? **Cause and Effect**

2. Read the word *tricked* on page 13. How did Little Turtle trick them? **Vocabulary**

3. Write about how this folktale helps explain nature. **Write About Reading**

Genre Folktale

Compare Texts
Read why bears have short tails.

Why Bear Has a Short Tail

A Flanders Folktale
retold by Jackie Maloy
Illustrated by Sarah Dillard

One day, Bear saw Fox eating some fish.

He asked, "Where did you get the fish?"

Fox wanted to play a trick on Bear.

She took him to a hole in a frozen lake.

She said, "Put your tail in the hole. The fish will bite it. Then you'll have fish!"

Bear thanked Fox.

Fox left the lake.

Bear sat down. He put his tail in the water.

Soon, the hole froze over. He stood up. But his tail stayed in the ice! His tail was trapped!

That is why bears are born with short tails.

Make Connections
How does Bear lose his tail?
Essential Question

How do these two folktales explain something in nature? **Text to Text**

Focus on Literary Elements

Theme The theme is the message or lesson in a story.

What to Look for In the play, the author tells you why turtles live in water. Look for what Little Turtle did. How did he get away? What is the lesson?

Your Turn

With a partner, pick an animal. Now choose something about the animal to explain. Your idea should end with, "And that's why ..." Share your idea with the rest of the class.